S0-DOO-793

To:

From:

7 Reasons to be Grateful You're the Mother of a

tweenager

Sheila Michaels

New Leaf Press
A Division of New Leaf Publishing Group

7 Reasons to be Grateful You're the Mother of a Tweenager

First Printing: December 2006

For information write: New Leaf Press, Inc., P.O. Box 726, Green Forest, AR 72638.

ISBN-13: 978-0-89221-651-2
ISBN-10: 0-89221-651-4
Library of Congress Catalog Number: 2006937325

Cover and Interior Design: LeftCoast Design, Portland, OR 97219
Printed in Italy

For information regarding author interviews, please contact the publicity department at (870) 438-5288.

Please visit our website for other great titles:
www.newleafpress.net

table of contents

1   gratefulness means we get a do-over day   9

2   gratefulness says a sense of humor is the best medicine   17

3   gratefulness means we are thankful that God has a plan   27

4   gratefulness means we are thankful for the people in our lives   35

5   gratefulness means we thank God for the job   45

6   gratefulness means we thank God for our strengths and weaknesses   55

7   gratefulness means we thank God for the journey   63

Dedicated to. . .

To my mom and dad who taught me that raising children
    requires a strong faith in God, the capacity to have fun,
    and a good sense of humor as they often muddle
    through their lives.

To my sister Dawn who listens when I have a parental
    breakdown and never judges. You are truly one of my
    best friends.

A united front is critical as children will often attempt to
    divide and conquer their parents. Thank you to my
    husband Cal for standing with me and creating a solid
    foundation for our kiddos to build their lives upon—we
    are an "awesome" team.

Finally, to my son Jordan and my daughter Sarah; God
    blessed me when each of you came into my life and I
    was forever changed. I am so proud to be "your" mom!

I love you all for the "many gifts" you have brought to my
    life—thank you!

CHAPTER 1

Gratefulness

means we get a

do-over day

The only real mistake is the one
from which we learn nothing.

John Powell

ith so many days in a child's life and so many
mistakes made as we muddle through the murky
waters of motherhood, it is difficult for one to
determine which day to eliminate, especially with soooooo
many blunders to choose from. For me, however, the choice
is simple. Don't get me wrong, I too have a myriad to choose
from, but one stands out as the one time I wish I had an

eraser, a rewind, an oh-my-God-please-tell-me-I-did-not-just-say-that-out-loud. After all, *"Speak when you are angry—and you will make the best speech you'll ever regret"*—Laurence J. Peter.

In my opinion, the individual who said "sticks and stones may break my bones, but words will never hurt me" was oblivious to the phenomenal power of words. He was probably the deaf bully lumbering across the playground wielding a stick and a few stones, frightening the other children, all the while oblivious to the vicious words that they whispered behind his back. Simply put, words have the power to cut like a knife and ultimately leave permanent scars, and unfortunately, as women, many of us have mastered the art of "word-fencing."

My daughter Sarah was at "the top-of-the-middle" or an

eighth grader; in the Michaels household, this grade was not a pinnacle for either child. By eighth grade, there is an egotistical, condescending, pompous attitude that manages to permeate a tweenager's entire being. However, for girls, between the verbal sparring with their friends and the child body that has grown boobs, there is an "I am now the woman of the house" attitude that follows her home each day. Their tongues are wicked, and moms often become targets where they are "blessed" to be the bulls-eye … woohooooo!

I remember one particular night as if it were yesterday … the memory is seared into my heart to serve as a reminder of the immense power of a solitary word. I picked Sarah up from practice and she was ornery—the bull's-eye on my face must have been blinking shades of neon, because target practice had begun! We only live three miles from town, but the ride felt like

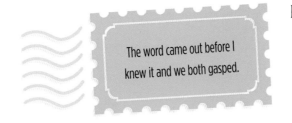

The word came out before I knew it and we both gasped.

an eternity. I let Sarah vent about the atrocities of her life for mile one, then offered motherly advice in mile two, and listened to her berate me until the end of mile three when I finally had enough. The word came out of my mouth before I knew it and we both gasped. I stopped the car and told her to walk the last 300 feet to our doorstep so I could cry and pray for God's guidance on how to handle the gaping wound I knew I had inflicted on Sarah's tender spirit.

We were both hurting when Sarah came trudging through the front door. The words spoken to me often by my mother echoed in my mind. I could hear her tender voice saying, "Into your hands, oh God" and that's where I found the strength to deal with the aftermath. Parents make mistakes; many of them, in fact. It was a sign to me that I was raising my daughter with God's grace when she came to me with open arms and forgave me. The incident remains in my heart as a reminder of the power of one little word to permanently etch a mark on a spirit, but also the power of God's incredible sacrifice . . . his Child for our forgiveness.

CHAPTER 2

Gratefulness

says a sense of humor is

the best medicine

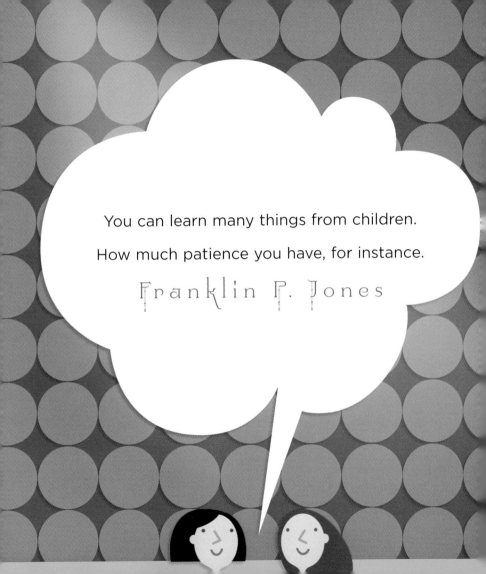

od has a sense of humor. In the course of my

life, I have seen this illustrated in many facets,

typically when I do not want to truly give myself

to God, but rather want to remain in control. A scowl will

often follow a "That's not funny, God" followed by a learning

moment. God's humor is clearly mirrored in the life of a

tween. Thankfully He gives us the strength to deal with them through faith. However, the bizarre, universal norms for munchkins of these ages are sooooooo frustrating that, for parents, the only thing that one *can* do is try to find the absurdity in the situations that continually arise, utter a "That's not funny, God," and laugh, too. The only alternative is to blow spit bubbles in the corner and admit defeat. Moms of future, up-and-coming tweenagers, brace yourself; you are in for a spiritual version of *Comedy Central*!

Moms, you need to have a sense of humor as your child grapples for a new vocabulary to adequately describe the world through their own eyes. Sometimes that means helping them along and frantically searching the archives of your own

Tweenagers forget
almost EVERYTHING . . .

mind as you try to make sense of what is being said, much like when they were learning their first words. For example, my son Jordan went to Bible camp where the girls stuck "snap-ons" all over the outside of the boy's cabin. Snap-ons . . . hmmmm, in our neck of the woods, Snap-on is a brand of tools and I was 100 percent sure that was not what the boy was talking about. Snap-ons, snap-ons, SNAP-ONS® . . . you mean, tampons? HYSTERICAL for me, but it led to another not-so-funny discussion for him. Amusement followed by a foundational, teachable moment perfectly depicts God's sense of humor.

Tweenagers forget almost EVERYTHING and both of my children were conformers to the norm. Our middle school has attempted to help parents and teachers cope with the temporary brain loss by providing students with planners that tell parents

what is due and when; however, the planner is pointless when . . .
you guessed it, they forget it. Not only do they forget their
homework, they also forget their gym clothes, their swimsuits,
their tennis shoes, their jackets, the time, and various important,
mandatory meetings (all of these more than once). This
forgetfulness is not funny; it is exasperating and exhausting.
In fact, I swear that I wore out a set or two of tires just driving
to the middle school with a surplus of essential forgotten
items. As parents approach the school secretary, there is a
look of empathy as the forgotten treasure is deposited for
the respective student. Usually the counter is full of deposits,
which is encouraging to parents because they know they are
not alone. Ironically, neither one of my children ever forgot a

social function that freed them from the parental constraints of home ... ODD! Humor and an environment in which parents feel empathy, compassion, and the fact they're not alone in their quest ... God's sense of humor.

Tweenagers continually push the envelope where rules are concerned. Your faith and theirs will be continually challenged. Steadfast boundaries are one of the keys to a solid Christian foundation; however, it is also handy to have a state trooper for a husband. Retrieving kids in their father's squad car is not only effective ... it's HILARIOUS! This humor comes in the form of an opportunity for parents to emphasize boundaries and create a unified front ... God's sense of humor.

You have to have a sense of humor when that one boy

that every girl is dreaming about doesn't even know your daughter exists. Or when you are assuring them that someday they will develop like the other boys and girls their age. Or when your child purchases some inappropriate, downloaded material from his best friend and gets caught by his father. Or when your child invites a "few" friends over and you end up with more munchkins than you know what to do with. There is always humor in the situation, typically with "teachable" moments intermingled with "learning" moments for both parents and tweens ... God's sense of humor. Proof that

"A sense of humor . . . is necessary armor. Joy in one's heart and some laughter on one's lips is a sign that the person down deep has a pretty good grasp of life" —Hugh Sidey.

Gratefulness

means we are thankful that

God has a plan

od graced our family with height. We are not vertically challenged, thus we anticipated that both Jordan and Sarah would be tall. When Jordan told us that he wanted to play basketball, both his father and I were excited. Almost immediately, Jordan loved being part of a team and he would come home each day wound up from practice. In fact, he was a legend in his own mind and we were excited to watch this newfound basketball "phenomenon" at his very first game.

On game day, Cal and I trotted off to proudly take our places with the other parents firmly planted on the sidelines. I smiled as I watched him saunter (yes, I said saunter) out onto the court. He spotted us and waved . . . *too cute*, I thought, and I proudly waved back. Then the usual pre-game lay-ups and free throws started. I focused on my gangly, smiling son and intently watched as he did his "thannnnggg."

Okay, I thought,

The game mattered to Sarah. She loved the competition, the fight, and the win . . .

this is just warm ups; it will get better. After all, there was one time that basketball almost reached the hoop. But it didn't get better; in fact, it actually got worse. He simply could not run, dribble, and shoot all at the same time . . . it was awful! I even saw a few sympathetic looks from other parents whose children actually did have some athletic abilities. Cal and I telepathically conveyed what the other was thinking. We did not have to worry about having the next "famous" basketball star; in fact, we were pretty sure that Jordan would become all too familiar with the bench before his "career" was done. When the game ended, Jordan bopped over, all smiles, and all the way home he bragged about his "skills," saying "Did you see it when I . . . ?" The game really did not matter to Jordan. He loved the practice, the camaraderie, and the team ... God graced him with the ability to dream.

We were prepared by the time Sarah joined basketball. She too was excited to play the game but never really talked much about practice or what she did there. When it came time to watch her first game, Cal and I again were planted firmly on the sidelines with the other parents. Again, I waved as she sprinted (yes, I said sprinted) out onto the court. Then came the time for the usual pre-game lay-ups and free throws. Her dad and I both sat up in our seats a little. One went in the hoop and another and another and another ... hmmmmm. *It's only the pre-game*; I fought the urge to get excited. Then came the actual game and I found myself clapping as she snatched the ball, dribbled down the court,

shot, and scored—it went in! Cal
and I looked at each other in
disbelief. As we turned our eyes
toward the court, Sarah stole
the ball, took off toward the
hoop again, shot, and scored—
it went in again! The game mattered
to Sarah. She loved the competition, the fight, and
the win … God graced her with determination.

God has a plan for Jordan and Sarah. He graced each of
them with special gifts that will allow that path to unfold. After
all, the big picture is still being gracefully painted with intricate
brush strokes on the canvas that is their lives.

Gratefulness

means we are thankful

for the people in our lives

ruly there should be an instruction manual for raising an adolescent tweenage girl; perhaps it could be called *Daughters for Dummies*. I think that title pretty well sums up my feelings of inadequacy when it comes to raising Sarah. The book could be an instruction manual of sorts with chapters such as: *Raging Estrogen Levels: The Duck and Cover Method for the 180° Mood Swing; Changing Bodies; Yes, Honey, I Promise They Will*

Grow; I Love You Mom, Now Get Away My Friends are Looking; Boys (*need*
I say more?), and most importantly, *Your Daughter Wants to be Popular:*
Run for Your Life Cuz it's Gonna Get Ugly. It is good that I have a
strong background and faith, because *nothing* prepared me
for the dynamic of the girl/girl relationship.

...an adolescent girl has raging hormones that can send her from zero to ugly in less than 3.5 seconds...

Now, if it isn't
bad enough that an
adolescent girl has
raging hormones
that can send her
from zero to ugly in less than 3.5 seconds, or anatomy that
simply refuses to grow while others attempt to beg theirs to
stop, she now has added boys into the mix and, with their fangs

showing, many girls are out for blood—their prey . . . their friends, best friends, or perhaps some unsuspecting soul that still holds out a desperate hope for being infamously popular. The elusive quest for popularity reared its nasty head on Sarah's thirteenth birthday.

Sarah begged us to have her first boy/girl party. Now, this was a monumental event in the Michaels' household as the "B" word is almost equated with a swear word in my husband's eyes. The party was to take place at a local water park and nearly forty tweenagers were invited to share in the festivities. The dialog between my daughter and I was grueling, like an incessant toothache. "No mom, I *have* to invite her or the boys will not come. It doesn't matter if I *really* like her, cuz they won't come otherwise. She hasn't been that mean *this* week. Mooooooooom! THEY WON'T COME IF SHE DOES NOT COME . . . ." This rally of mother-daughter sparring went back and forth until, against my better judgment, the invitations were sent out or hand-delivered to the "popular posse" and a few choice others.

Throughout the next few days there was a barrage of calls from individuals planning to attend. Well, I can admit when I am wrong and all seemed to be going as Sarah had planned. My sister Dawn and her daughters Mariah and Paige had opted to come up and provide assistance and moral support. After all, forty hungry tweenagers with raging hormones may have been more than this mom could tolerate; I could scarcely handle one.

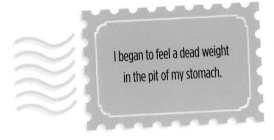

I began to feel a dead weight in the pit of my stomach.

The evening started out a little slow. One girl, two, three, and four ... I began to relax a little bit and thank God. Giggles, talk about boys, and who was coming seemed to be the primary topics of conversation that pervaded the room. *Hmmmm . . . where are the rest of them?* I began to feel a dead weight in the pit of my stomach. I knew this feeling and I hoped my daughter would never have to feel it. My heart broke when I realized not only were the boys not coming, neither were the "popular" girls. This was it—four girls, my sister, and her girls for a grand total ... drum roll, please ... of

EIGHT! It was sabotage and Sarah was the victim. One popular girl told another and another and it worked its way through the proverbial grapevine—lesson learned.

Now, I have to admit that I was very grateful for those individuals who showed up to celebrate with Sarah as the party, although intimate, turned out to be a hit. We splashed, swam,

careened down the waterslides, shared stories in the hot tub, looked for cute boys, and managed to put a pretty good dent in the food for forty. Often we are blessed with friends that come into our lives and we believe that they are important until we see others who mirror what we *think* we want to be. Sometimes we waver from those initial friendships and our moral and ethical values in a quest for popularity among the masses of our peers. God challenges us in our life's journey to search for the meaning inside the times that are the most difficult. Sarah found that meaning and discovered true friendship.

So the final chapter in my *Daughters for Dummies* would be *Friends and Books: Choose Carefully*. After all, "*I am a part of all that I have read*"—John Kieren.

CHAPTER 5

Gratefulness

means we thank God

for the job

W hen my son Jordan entered middle school, I felt the
same way I do when I am gazing at the monstrous
lurching, twisting, loop-de-loops of a newly discovered
roller coaster—terrified and excited at the same time. On
orientation day, I received an informative brochure about
what to expect from your preadolescent. I flippantly perused
the pages full of some "expert" snippets of advice and plopped

> He looked so angelic sitting at attention as the principal talked to his captive audience—I was so proud.

it in the "will file in the trash when I get home" pile. I remember chuckling at the references to hormones, forgetfulness, irrational behavior, and a barrage of "undesirable" characteristics associated with "raising a preadolescent." Hmmmm . . . I thought as I looked at the wide-eyed innocence of my new sixth-grader. He looked so angelic sitting at attention as the principal talked to his captive audience—I was so proud. I had barely gotten the thought into my brain when Jordan turned toward me and rolled his eyes as if the ride was boring and he wanted to get off. His body language spoke volumes and I thought I saw the sprouting of little horns in his shock of blonde hair. Instantly I changed my mind to file the brochure in the "might need to read later" pile.

To say that I was totally unprepared for being a mom of a preadolescent is an understatement. It is like saying that one is prepared for the extreme climbs and falls of a roller coaster; you simply cannot adequately prepare. Jordan started the year in a flurry of locker combinations, horrendously tooting on a band instrument for the first time, and discovering girls, all mixed in with a tish of testosterone for good measure. However, there was something new: Jordan now hated the bus.

After a dare, my typically mild mannered little boy threw a rock at the bus window.

I was unaware of how deeply his loathing went until we received a call from the bus

garage. After a dare, my typically mild-mannered little boy

threw a rock at the bus window. A dare ... he got back at the

bus all right ... NOT! I said a little prayer and found myself

frantically searching for that blasted brochure for a little

light reading for additional support. Jordan ended up paying

for the bus window and getting grounded with no time off for
good behavior. Lesson learned? NOPE!

Jordan had
just finished his
punishment when
I received a call
from the principal,

I ran my fingers through my hair
and told God that I wanted to
get off of the ride … NOW!

who reported that Jordan had poked holes in a bus seat with
a paper clip. *Who does that?* I thought. I ran my fingers through
my hair and told God that I wanted to get off of the ride …
NOW! I said a big prayer, pulled myself together, and trotted
into school to have a heart-to-heart in the principal's office.
My meek little boy/man-child was sitting with his head hung

and eyes to the floor. The tears threatened to spill over as he looked up into my eyes—my heart broke and there was a groaning in the pit of my stomach. God blessed me with this child and this is my job. I swallowed the tears, prayed for strength, and I held firm. Jordan was sentenced to three weeks of cleaning the very buses he detested, but he did it and did so willingly. The lesson was learned and I was proud of him. So while I still love the wild and crazy adventure of riding the roller coaster of motherhood, I still have to remember that, like adults, our preadolescents *are not human beings on a spiritual journey [but rather] spiritual beings on a human journey"*—Stephen Covey.

Gratefulness

means we thank God

for our strengths

and weaknesses

N o mother likes to discipline her child; however, there are valuable, "teachable" moments when determining what is and what is not acceptable behavior. At that crossroad, moms have to choose which path will better serve her child as they move forward into their spiritual development. My son Jordan was renowned for asking to do inappropriate things when I was on the phone, had company, or was otherwise busy. Typically he would ask to go someplace or have a friend over and would beg until, in exasperation, I would cave in. It annoyed me, but no mother really likes to discipline her child and I was no exception to the rule—this was my weakness.

> Now he tromped, raised his voice, and acted atrociously in front of my company.

I saw a saying once that said "Raising children is like being slowly pecked to death by a chicken." I wonder if God feels that way sometimes. I know that I felt like that chicken one afternoon when I had company. It was not surprising when Jordan began his relentless begging to have his buddy come over. I was supposed to do I-don't-know-what with my company, and leave her with I-don't-know-who, for I-don't-know-how-long, while I ran into town and got a friend for him to occupy his time. Needless to say, I said no. End of discussion?—Nope. He huffed and puffed, begged and begged to no avail. Again, more firmly this time, I said no. End of discussion?—Not yet. Now he stomped, raised his voice, and acted atrociously in front of my company. Now I was not only angry, I was embarrassed at his behavior. Again, I firmly said no. He retorted with "I hate you, mom!" Line crossed. I was hurt and angry. As I saw it, I had two choices. The first was to allow this behavior to continue and perhaps have him say that to me in the future or to deal with it head on. I opted for the latter.

Upstairs we went, into the bathroom for a "teeny-tiny-enough-for-a-taste" dollop of soap, a minimal mouth washing, and his punishment was over. End of discussion?—Nope! He screamed at me, "You're the meanest mom in the world!" Yup, there it was. I already knew it,

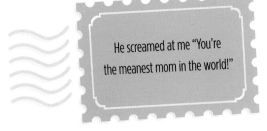

He screamed at me "You're the meanest mom in the world!"

but now it had adequately been verbalized. WOW, *what should I do with that?* I thought. Again, I was at a crossroads. I rarely spanked either of my kids, but Jordan got a spanking and was sent to his room to think about what he had done.

When I finally made my way downstairs, I was again embarrassed at the realization that my company had witnessed the whole nasty scenario; however, I acknowledged the incident and moved on. I was thankful for God's strength to follow through with Jordan's punishment, and eventually he made his way downstairs and apologized to my visitor and me. Jordan never again told me that he hated me, and even if he thought I was the meanest mother in the world, he never verbalized it again—lesson learned. One needs to remember that in a child's life *"there is so much to teach, and the time goes so fast"*—Erma Bombeck.

CHAPTER 7

Gratefulness

means we thank God

for the journey

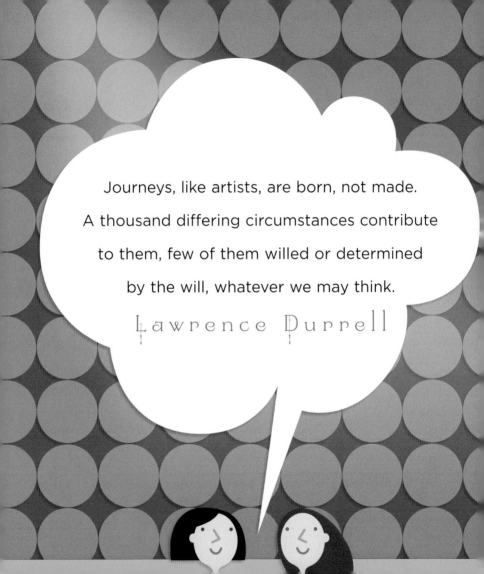

Journeys, like artists, are born, not made.
A thousand differing circumstances contribute
to them, few of them willed or determined
by the will, whatever we may think.

Lawrence Durrell

God's delicate touch can be seen in the lives of our children. I often think about my own with awe and wonder at Him, especially when I consider how two children who come from the same gene pool can be so totally different. *Sheila, the great pontificator!* This from the mother who thought her children would not fight because they were not the same gender. Ahhhhh, the wonder of being a new mom,

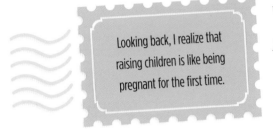

Looking back, I realize that raising children is like being pregnant for the first time.

then reality slaps you with a wet noodle as your firstborn screams at you to "Put her back!" The perfect illusion is successfully eradicated.

Looking back, I realize that raising children is like being pregnant for the first time. When you first find out that you are pregnant, you are ecstatic. This is much the same feeling as when you see your baby for the first time. It is beyond words and one can truly feel the hands of God when first holding "your" child.

When pregnancy begins, many women experience morning sickness. After a child is born, there is also a feeling of nausea as one realizes how much would be lost if something happened to the precious life now sleeping in the crib.

As one moves forward in the pregnancy, the cravings and desires begin to have things that sometimes are unattainable. For me that was Kentucky Fried Chicken's mashed potatoes and gravy—not available in a town of 500 people. Wanting things we cannot have is also experienced by toddlers. It is frustrating and, on occasion, whining occurs in a quest to fill the desire.

As the life grows within a mother's womb, there is a feeling of connectedness and she is allowed a couple of months of "coasting." This for me was much the same as when my children were between the ages of 4 and 8. There was not a lot of

conflict and I believe it was God's way of

allowing me to regain my energy as

we moved into "preadolescence."

As the baby grows in its

mother's womb, Mom

becomes more and

more uncomfortable.

For me, this was how I

felt when my children

became tweenagers.

The whole period of

time was trial, error,

troubleshooting,

praying... and did I mention, praying? I was totally out of my

comfort zone just like I was when the child in my stomach

opted to do loop-de-loops just for the fun of it.

Finally, an expectant mother experiences a period of time before the baby

> Moms wait up at night for their "babies" to get home. They panic if they are one minute late, sometimes even if they are not.

arrives when she is so uncomfortable that she can scarcely

breathe. During this time I was up at night. I worried about

my delivery, whether I would be a good mom, what I'd do if

something happened... basically everything that was beyond

my control. Today, you guessed it—welcome to the world of

teenagers, cars, boys, girls, friends, drinking, drugs—the praying on this leg of the journey will be continual. Moms wait up at night for their "babies" to get home. They panic if they are one minute late, sometimes even if they are not. They worry about whether they are safe or whether something happened, because they know it can—and the feeling leaves them breathless. I gained so much of God's grace when Jordan and Sarah were born, and they are intertwined in my life's journey—simply put, they complete me.

So moms, I leave you with this, *"Your children will become what you are; so be what you want them to be,"* after all, *"having children makes you no more a parent than having a piano makes you a pianist"*—David Bly and Michael Levine

We're thankful you've chosen to explore

7 Reasons to be Grateful You're the Mother of a Tweenager.

If these essays have made you recall your own for-better-or-worse moments, take a few minutes to write some thoughts to perhaps share with your child(ren) sometime... like after they have their *own* kids.

How Many Do-Over Days Can We Have?

Sometimes during a long string of seemingly wasted days, we long for meaning, purpose, and some guarantee this child-rearing gig will turn out positively. Is there a time you can look back on, now from a different perspective, when the dreariness of day-to-day family duties produced a bit of hope after a long, dry spell?

When Your Sense of Humor is Buried Beneath Your Laundry...

Immediately following 9/11, New York Mayor Rudy Giuliani suggested we needed to find a way to laugh again—while we're still crying. Some might suggest this applies to motherhood as well. Can you recall some times when laughter gave way to tears ... and tears gave way to laughter?